Prayers & Run-on Sentences

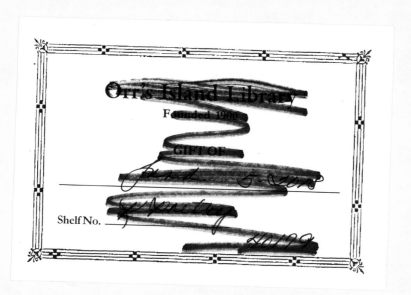

Prayers &
Run-on Sentences

Poems

Stuart Kestenbaum

DEERBROOK EDITIONS

PUBLISHED BY
Deerbrook Editions
P.O. Box 542
Cumberland, Maine 04021-0542
207-829-5038

FIRST EDITION

ISBN: 0-9712488-6-9
978-0-9712488-6-1

On the cover:
Fallen, monotype by Susan Webster
On the title page:
Heaven, monotype by Stuart Kestenbaum and Susan Webster

BOOK DESIGN BY *Jeffrey Haste*
MANUFACTURED BY WALCH PRINTING, PORTLAND, ME

Contents

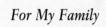

For My Family

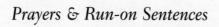

Prayers & Run-on Sentences

Benediction

Heaven knows
where you'll go
once you
get started,
only that
the rain
will wake
your heart
and something
will sprout
within you, something
you can't
name and the earth
of your body
will welcome
it home.

Prayer

Our problem—may I include you?—is that we
don't know how to start, how to just close
our eyes and let something dance between
our hearts and our lips, we don't know how
to skip across the room only for the joy of the leap.
We walk, we run, but what happened to the skip
and its partner, the gallop, the useless and imaginary
way we could move through space, the horses we
rode before we knew how to saddle up, before we
had opinions about everything and just loved
the wind in our faces and the horizon in our eyes.

April Prayer

Just before the green begins there is the hint of green
a blush of color, and the red buds thicken
the ends of the maple's branches and everything
is poised before the start of a new world,
which is really the same world
just moving forward from bud
to flower to blossom to fruit
to harvest to sweet sleep, and the roots
await the next signal, every signal
every call a miracle and the switchboard
is lighting up and the operators are
standing by in the pledge drive we've
all been listening to: Go make the call.

To Alice, Who Taught Me About Poems

I remember when we would stay up all night
heading down to the village to watch the baker

make the doughnuts, the greasy 'O's rising
miraculously in the oil. I'm sure he was wondering

why jerked-up college kids would come down the hill to visit him:
He was at work, while we were at discovery. Some jobs

can be discoveries, not like the ones famous scientists make
but like those I made before I visited you that summer.

I was working in the gas station, learning to stop the pump
just right on the dollar, not going over by a penny, or cleaning

the windshields perfectly with the squeegee, the water
running down like a light show on the shadow of the dash board.

I hitchhiked from Boston to Maine to visit you at your cottage,
getting a long ride in a hippie's recycled delivery van past the hulks

of the schooners rotting in the harbor in Wiscasset, past
the souvenirs in Perry's Nut House in Belfast,

until I was dropped off on route 15, still 40 miles away,
in the mosquito-filled dusk near the humming and flickering

lights of the gas station, like an Edward Hopper painting come to life.
How is it when night comes on we can feel so alive?

The darkness is surrounding us and we're standing
with our hopeful thumbs out waiting for a ride.

Dawn Prayer

This morning I wake early to see if I can discover
wild animals who are busy before dawn because this is a way
of knowing that there are other lives in the world, owls living
and breathing in the dark pine and whatever else lives in the dawn
and is moving freely as the train whistle is blowing off in the distance,
which is almost now a forgotten sound of a bygone era, technology
becoming quaint through change, and all around us there is nothing
that is not changing in its own time, the billions of years for the rock,
the hours for the microbe, the years for the person, the life in the middle
of the song, the pen that runs out of ink before the story is finished
and we need to remember what we can.

Driving and Going to Work Prayer

Driving across the causeway this morning
I saw the sun rising, only it wasn't a blinding-
in-your-eyes yellow sun, it was a huge
red ball coming up through layers of stratus clouds,
a red sun as if it were a science fiction movie
and we had landed on a planet that was almost like earth,
but there were other planets circling us, other suns,
and that's how my morning began, looking for something
miraculous that is always there, the same way Cheryl
was cooking breakfast for 100 people and didn't want
to leave the eggs until they began to scramble themselves
into yellow clusters and became breakfast
and who wouldn't want to wait for that because that's
when we are transformed, when we are changed,
and we are ourselves but also becoming something
different, something we didn't know that begins
to change itself, something that's coming, arriving,
returning, like a multiple choice question when the answer
is all of the above, all of the above.

Prayer in the Strip Mall, Bangor, Maine

The week after Thanksgiving and the stores are decked out
for holiday shopping including a TJ Maxx where what was
once too expensive loses its value and attracts us, there is a
store with a big yellow banner proclaiming GIANT BOOK SALE,
a seasonal operation of remaindered books, which doesn't mean
that the books aren't good, only that the great machinery
of merchandising didn't engage its gears in quite the right way
and I buy two books of poetry and am leaving the store, the first snowstorm
of the winter on the way and as I get to the glass double doors
a bearded man with a cane is entering, he has been walking
with a woman who is continuing on to another store and he
has the look that could make him either eccentrically brilliant
or just plain simple and as I open the door and he opens the other side
he turns and says "I love you," not to me but calling back to his
friend who is departing, only he's said it looking at me, closest
to me, which is unintended love, random love, love that
should be spread throughout the world, shouted in our ears for free.

Pastoral

The fields make a harmony of the rusted
remains of cars, the boulders left behind
by the glaciers, the styrofoam cups
hung up in the underbrush,
the crows overhead. The barns join them
in this song. Empty of use, holding
only memories of cows and hay, they begin
to sag toward earth. On route 3, right after
the new acres of Bank of America
where telemarketers sow debt in the old fields,
the barn stands, like a rock in the river
of wind that erodes it everyday. To think
that wind and water, that famous partnership,
can take this down in a slow dismantling
of purpose, purposeful in itself because it
gets us back to the circle of beginning and ending.
Everything is headed that way, one day,
when it looks like death has just visited,
and there is more collapsed than standing,
the posts and beams that were once the trees
of the forest, fallen a second time,
and we all know what sound that makes,
the sound that rings in the ears of philosophers,
those guys who are always around at the end
trying to make sense of things.
They're out there listening now
to the steady March wind,
which has the cold of February
and the promise of April,
each its own story
told again and again.

Headache Prayer

I wake with a headache and watch as the blue jay
who yesterday had a stick in its beak continues
to build its nest and I see it fly from the maples that grew up
in the brush, over the roof to wherever the nest will be,
and for the blue jay it's the start of a day that is in the present
looking toward the future informed by the instinct of the past,
from wing to tree to nest to offspring to wing and my pulse
throbs in my head and down into my chest, an ancient
drum that is beating in everything, in the sap in the tree,
in the seed in the ground, in the wind on the horizon. Amen.

Walking Prayer

I begin my day by walking down the road, the snow bank growing
on the side, the sand and exhaust grime settling on the shoulders
so that it looks like it's the ground reappearing and I'm watching
my footsteps careful not to step into the path of a pick-up truck
when I see on the ground uncovered in the slush,
a pack of Marlboro Lights, a white pack,
maybe this is a wintertime pack, and I think in the spring how so much
more of what has littered the roadside will be revealed, this pack now
the only manifestation, and how we love the snow because it covers
everything, revealing the outline of the landscape but also hiding
the blemishes and we can imagine a world that's new again everyday
and isn't that what I want to imagine when I turn on the radio and make
the coffee, a routine that's so familiar I don't remember not doing it,
and I hear the same old news even if it's new news, which I forget as soon
as I hear it, or maybe later in the day begin to recount it for someone else
and transform it sightly just like the kids' game of telephone,
and so each day begins, each sedimentary day like snow piling up
or silt in some ancient riverbed, layered and packed down upon itself.

Litany

Bless us with the first breath of morning. Bless the packet of seeds for the garden, shaking like a shaman's rattle in prayer. Bless us with spare change in our pockets to give to the homeless, bless us with a heart that has been serviced by the mechanic, bless us with good tires on the icy road. Bless us so that we're not just covering our own asses, but weeping for the rest of the world. Bless our tears so that they irrigate the land for the starving, that there be no more drought. Bless us with one idea after another that we might sort out the good from the bad, bless us with free lunches and subscriptions, bless us with a winter storm so big that it closes everything down for a week and we can find ourselves at the beginning of time. Bless us with water, bless us with light, bless us with darkness, and bless us with language. Bless our tongues that we can speak. Bless our cars so they start. Bless our computers so that they may connect to the internet and bring us the news of the universe. Bless Robert Bly and Gloria Steinem, bless all the worn-out athletes whose bodies are falling apart, bless the tides twice a day and the moon every month. Bless the sun, bless us as we are blessing you for this is a two-way street after all and we're in this thing together. Bless mass transit and the first cup of coffee. Sing o ye frost heaves and icy patches, praise the spruce trees all crowded together, the crows in the trees flying heaven-ward and earthward, flying everywhere in between. Bless the night with its constellations that we have dreamed up. Bless our stories that they may somehow be true, for this is all we have. Bless all creatures great and small and the basket makers who weave together a framework to hold emptiness. Bless the empty spaces that are within us, between each cell in our body and in the vast distances between each cell. Bless each cell, which is its own universe, ready to divide, split in two, and make more than enough.

Ancestor Prayer

The grass is covered with the first crust
of icy snow so that walking across it
I can see the footsteps of those who
have gone before me, like following the paths
of ancestors as if there is some solace
and sanctuary in following those who have
preceded us and I walk to the meditation hall
where high windows show only the branches
and not the trunks of the trees and in this way
we're not seeing the source, but we know
it's there because it supports the branches
that hold the leaves, which today are no longer
there, fallen to the ground, blown into the banks
of the river, carried away on wind and water.

School Days

The blank notebooks for school never turn out the way you think
they will, how full of possibility they appear at the beginning of the year,
the three-ring binder, the multi-color divider pages, the small notebook
to write down all your assignments. This year is going to be different,
you think, starting with the blank slate, the possibilities that algebra and
trigonometry will be made clear, that the Civil War and Nicholas Biddle
will interest you for ten months, that no doodles will take up pages.
What if you walk into class the first day and all your teacher says
is "pay attention" and she walks you outside. You sit and look
at the patch of grass next to the road, with bottle caps, cigarette butts,
microbes, earthworms, the tiny white roots, the seed pods of maples
edging earthward. Paying attention would be the only subject.
The bell rings and you spend an hour looking into someone's eyes,
the bell rings again and you spend an hour examining someone's heart,
the bell rings again and you take off all your clothes and look
at yourself in the mirror. This is the new school. You throw
the notebook pages out the window and they flutter to the ground.
Someone in another class observes the snow fall of the blank page,
the piling up of nothingness on the ground. For the class picnic
everyone fasts. For the class dance you make a circle, you ask your elders
to join the janitor and the school secretary, the security guard,
your grandparents and little brother and dance in a circle.
Outside it's spring and the school year is closing down on itself.
The janitors are sweeping with their long push brooms,
the dust of history and quadratic equations, the grammar of your life.
Whether you lie down or lay down doesn't matter. You know you want
to sleep, deeply, and wake up in the world where hope is alive, where
words whisper their stories to you, where the ticking clock of the school,
the one with Roman Numerals, has sprung free, has exploded
into the parking lot and is showering all those precious minutes
and seconds on the ground. Outside someone is paying attention
and scoops them up. She'll go home for the summer
and make something beautiful from it,
some suit of light to wander in.

Water Prayer

And this morning I awoke to rain, which makes
its own rhythm on the window, and the world is full
of these rhythms, rhythm of water, rhythm of the heart,
which sounds like an underwater pump, the lub-dub
of all it knows, which is making all I know possible,
and on the roof rain falls and turns to hail, then snow,
then rain again, running down the shingles to the gutter,
the gathering up that makes rivers and lakes and oceans,
from cloud to drop to torrent, how nothing is lost.

Prayer for the Dead

The light snow started late last night and continued
all night long while I slept and could hear it occasionally
enter my sleep, where I dreamed my brother
was alive again and possessing the beauty of youth, aware
that he would be leaving again shortly and that is the lesson
of the snow falling and of the seeds of death that are in everything
that is born: we are here for a moment
of a story that is longer than all of us and few of us
remember, the wind is blowing out of someplace
we don't know, and each moment contains rhythms
within rhythms, and if you discover some old piece
of your own writing, or an old photograph,
you may not remember that it was you and even if it was once you,
it's not you now, not this moment that the synapses fire
and your hands move to cover your face in a gesture
of grief and remembrance.

Cape Cod Clothes Line

The world is full of useful things
like clothespins that can hold laundry
in place and let it be free at the same time,
let your pants and underwear
dance with the wind that is moving
around the world. In this simple way
a modest clothespin holds the world
together, makes an order that makes
harmony possible. A clothespin made
of wood in a small mill in Maine, turned
and sawed, all the hand's work to make
an object that lets you hold onto things.
Sometimes in our minds we're holding
onto life by our fingernails and we don't
want to slip away, Lord knows,
we want to hold on, hold onto the first
breath of morning, hold onto our place
in line, hold onto the planet, wobbling
slightly itself in the vastness of someone's
making. It's the simple things we're looking for,
relatives of the clothespin like the thumbtack
and its cousin, the push pin, that allow us
to back away and get some perspective,
or the nail, which allows us to join
together rooms, walls, houses, towns
held in place with such a small item,
a shaft of metal with a flattened end,
like divine lightning bolts placed just so.
But let's get back to our laundry,
which must be dry by now, after a morning
of fluttering, after a morning
of absorbing the dryness of the world,
a stiff new beginning of cleanliness.
Underneath the clothesline the grass that keeps
the far side of the dune in place. I look and see

Henry Beston walking down along the shore.
He's dead now and gets to wander his favorite
place, along Cape Cod, where he made his life
simple, where he watched the wind
and tide bring the world to the shore, where
he watches my laundry moving
like prayer flags in blue air.

Reunion Prayer

When I look at myself in the bathroom mirror
it would be no surprise to anyone but me that I don't appear the way
I remember, like seeing someone else at the high school reunion
and wondering what years lay between childhood and now,
when you find yourself in a nondescript hotel off route 46
in what used to be pasture and watch time unfold or watch it as it has
unfolded as if we're reading from the Book of Life, inscribed
by the Eternal One, which in a sense we are, including of course who
shall live and who shall die, who by fire and who by water, and we move
around the dance floor as if we're the same people but we've stepped
into other people's bodies—our parents, our ancestors—
and we're remembering how our feet move, we're remembering
songs that seem like they never went away even though they're long gone.

Dream Prayer

All night long the river runs alongside where I sleep
and my dreams are sluicing down the stone banks
and the last of the day's detritus, shaken out of my pockets,
is entering the water and on its way to the ocean
so when I wake to a day that has broken with mute
gray, the trucks rolling over the bridge, the rest
of my spent life will be downstream already, moving past
an abandoned mill, eddying up against the birches' roots
and becoming ice for the winter.

Prayer Before Coffee

When I rise in the blue day, downstairs the candle
lit in my brother's memory still burns on the stove
and I want to preserve this world without words,
not even one syllable to enter my waking, no thoughts
of how many days are filled with all the things
that I can tell myself, where I am the DJ of my own
talk radio, coming at you 24 hours a day with needless
advice. I think instead of last night's dream
of the endless droplets of water flooding the road,
washing over everything, stalling the UPS truck
so there can be no deliveries, so that only now is here.

Silence

after a monotype by Alan Magee

I wanted to stop talking.
I wanted to close my eyes and stitch my lips together
so that all I could do was remember.
I wanted to be a witness to all that was left
and all that had gone before.
I wanted my neurons to fire again and again inside
the silence of my skull and to listen for the tiny snaps
as they ignited with knowledge.
I wanted to stand outside for awhile, my eyes sealed to the day,
and only hear the enormous wind that carries grief in its throat.
I wanted to tremble with the sibilant air passing through my stitches.
I wanted to be wounded and healed at the same time.
I wanted to mark time on my face.
I wanted to weep, but not so anyone would see, but to feel
tears move down my face as if my flesh were its own geology.
I wanted to remember everything and hate nothing.
I wanted to feel the light of votive candles
flicker against my eyelids.
I wanted to hear the whispered prayers of people I never knew.
I wanted to stand so still that I could feel the electricity
of my body thrumming in my chest, that I could
feel your body as you walked past.
I wanted to feel you stand next to me, like two people saying grace
before the meal began. I couldn't eat if I wanted to. I just wanted
to feel the silence before gratefulness begins.
I wanted to feel the gratefulness of survival.
I wanted to remember this sewn-together world,
this patched and stitched world.
I wanted to breathe so that air was all I was thinking about.
I wanted to feel the air enter my lungs and escape through
my poorly mended skull. In that way the world would be
passing through me. In that way I could be a witness,
standing vigil. I would be joined to you and

you to me. I wanted to keep my mouth closed for a long time
and only dream of the next world.
I wanted to see a miracle on the inside of my eyes,
one that I could speak about without a tongue.
I stood and breathed. I stood and remembered.
I was rocking back and forth like someone praying.
I wanted to pray and I wanted my lips to move.

Prayer for Slowing Down

Today I've been watching the shadows move
across the white building that was once a barn
and now is used to store dishes and tables and chairs
because we have too much of everything and the windows
make a fine white line in the black reflection of glass, speckled
with new paint like ancient stars, and all day the shadows
have drawn themselves on the clapboards, and told the old
story of light, how it dances in our eyes and we praise it,
how it is fleeting: here, then gone, like the river
outside my window, all last night rumbling and thrashing,
fluid beyond imagination, transporting last year's leaves
and silt from forgotten fields.

Prayer for Going on a Journey

We start with the fog dampening
the trembling leaves, and I'm half
remembering a dream about putting
the truck in 4-wheel drive
to ascend a hill on a college campus
even though I haven't been inside
a classroom for years and even though
the road isn't icy this morning, it's
just a day with the first fallen leaves,
the ones from the weaker trees
the tired leaves of the old white birch
small yellow boats in a sea of grass.

Prayer for an Empty Mind

And what if we didn't stop at the point where we said *enough*
but kept on going, like a runner hitting his stride and reaching
a point that didn't seem possible, even as a new century begins
or a day, or how about those who keep track of things one
breath at a time, which is the increment that sustains us,
one breath at a time and one moment, only we string these
together, beads on a chain, in and out, in and out, until we are
looking at another morning or another year and are still breathing,
still forming thoughts in the foundries of our brains, casting
one after another, waiting for the quality-control inspector
to get on the job and start looking at these things
before we start shipping them out into the world.

Grief Arrives In Its Own Time

It doesn't announce itself or knock
on the door of your heart. Suddenly

it's right behind you
looking with great pity

at the back of your neck
and your shoulders on which

it spends days placing a burden
and lifting it. Grief arrives

in its own sweet time, *sweet*
because it lets you know that

you are alive, *time* because
what you are holding becomes

the only day there is: the sun stops
moving, the sky grows utterly quiet

and impossibly blue. Behind the blue
are the stars we can't see and beyond

the stars either dark or light,
both of which are endless.

Prayer for Dreams

The birds wake before you do in the dawn
when everything is still shadows and shapes
and you can hear the beating of their wings,
the call of a raven, only one raven, when yesterday
twenty or more wheeled in the sky, high above,
sometimes pairing off, barely moving their wings
to ride the air and you think how for the bird
beginning a day there is all wings and heat,
air and lift, and for you there is slowly remembering
dreams without wings, dreams that hang before you
like a ripe fruit to peck at and pull out its seeds.

Waking Prayer

When you wake in the morning with Expectation, not like she's
just visiting for coffee, but you actually slept with her and her
best friend, Responsibility, and you sit at a table before the sun
has come up and the three of you have can have a conversation and be
like good friends who go on vacation in the woods and have never
spent so much time together and you begin to notice
each other's annoying habits, how Responsibility is
always looking at his watch and Expectation does
this weird thing with her head, slowly moving side to side,
like she's always disappointed in what just happened,
so the three of you are sitting together and you can hear
your cheap wristwatch ticking loudly as if that's the heartbeat
of the world and outside the sparrows are chirping the light back
into the day and the pigeons are undulating in unison
in the brightening sky.

The Story of Rubber

after a sample box by Richard Marquis

Everything has its own story. Oil, coal, gas, flax, cotton, dinosaurs, Abraham Lincoln, George Washington, and Caesar. That's what school is all about. You learn each story until your head is full of stories and then you can wander out into the world. Jonas Salk has his story, Amelia Earhart has her story. Rubber has its own story too, the natives slitting the bark in the forest of Brazil and making a bouncing world, a rolling world, a world softened by the sap inside the tree. Trees have their stories too. Even stories have their stories. When rubber became scarce, I think because of the first World War, which has its own story, we began to make rubber from oil (that's two stories coming together) and that's how New Jersey was born. Rubber made games possible—basketball and football, and swim fins and the pink Spalding balls for all those games you could make up on your own. Each game has a story, you can create your own scenarios in your backyard, the last minute of the game, the last second of the game and if the game doesn't end the way you wanted it to, you can start over again. That's the best part of stories—you can be your own tailor, you can alter endings, you can be your own God and say 'Let there be hope' and there was or you can make a small perfect world, one that you can control with your language. You can make a world, but so can everyone else and after a while they're all bouncing against each other, like those rubber balls that were only used in school for kick ball, the game no one ever played for real, you knew it didn't have the weight, the dramatic tension, just that hollow-sounding rubber that you could hear resonate when you'd propel it with your foot or bounce it against the asphalt. There's an emptiness inside a ball like that. Not like the emptiness inside an atom but like the emptiness inside a tomb or a waiting room, the waiting rooms with the out-of-date magazines, the ones with the stories about Brad Pitt and Jennifer Aniston, the ones with the family that lost everything to some disaster, but carried on. It could have been you, it's the way the ball bounces, that random rubber sphere, not directed like the ball that helps you on sing-alongs, but like a planet of randomness, out of orbit, taking the long way home.

Prayer I Should Have Prayed Last Night

When I wake I am still carrying the night with me,
the trembling wind we are awash in, and the wind
outside howls or does what wind does, which is
not howl but knit trees and leaves together with clouds
and lash the sun together with the moon. I am only
imagining this because I haven't studied my science today
and so can't tell the truth of things, I can only tell
what I am making up at this moment when the darkness
departs like a wave receding, and the sea is absorbed
in the dense sand, which lightens as the water travels away,
the same way I lay awake in my bed last night, fear
washing over me and seeping into the mattress,
my vessel, my washed-up raft.

Blessing

Yesterday morning the first snow began to fall
and I was walking down the main street of town
on the way to do my laundry and a dense snowflake,
somewhere between hail and snow, landed on my lip,
which I didn't notice until my tongue moved across it
and it was as if I had gotten a small drink from heaven.
This morning the wind, which this time of year tears
through the world, over and around buildings
as if they are stones in a stream, blew the door open.
My back was to the door so that I thought guests
had arrived, winter visitors who would stamp
their boots and hold the freezing air close to their skin.

Theology

God isn't watching everything, seeing who's been bad
or good so be good for goodness sake, God is weaving and sewing,
God is mending and repairing, what with so much that is
tattered and frayed. God is remembering the past by sewing it
into the future. God is making lace and making samplers,
so many samplers the creator has made, one for each moment.
Every sampler has its own language, its own colors, its own
chemistry, and its own music. God knows all the songs
and all the elements and at night she sings the world to bed.
Sometimes she'll sing whole new worlds into being,
just by naming the stuff of it. Other times he'll
get out the broom and sweep up
the dust of the last universe, the grit and fluff,
the shavings and the crumbs, the crumpled papers,
and make a new world. That's the one we're living in now
and that's why it feels new and ancient at the same time.
We begin our world where the last one ends.
God has a barn raising and we're all working
with the creator together, pushing up
one wall at a time. People have begun to till the earth,
reverently dropping the seeds in the furrows. God is becoming
the seeds, remembering all the way back to the beginning of seed,
which is a place where light could sleep,
sleep and dream and then awaken, and become what it needs to be
in this world, which is being created and re-created this minute.
Let us all bless it.

Spring Prayer

The white that appears to be the last remnant
of the snow in the woods is a plastic trash bag
snagged in the undergrowth, as natural a phenomenon
as anything, considering all things come
from something of this earth– you, me, plastic bags,
pebbles, and sand– and we're all moving at our own pace
somewhere, the where of which we haven't figured out yet
and never will, the some of which is the treasure chest
of all we've accumulated, how lovingly we hold
these artifacts in our minds: the photo, the book,
the jewel, the sorrow, the green shoot piercing
last year's fallen leaf.

Prayer of Light

When the clouds are moving across the sky so that an
immense wall of dark gray cumulus clouds are front-lit
by the sun, then everything is alight for the moment
with a white gold, and in the village the regular geometry
of the small Greek Revival steeple on the church
that is no longer consecrated is illuminated, surrounded
by blue-green Vermont mountains, and you are
sitting in a valley, an ancient valley in which this wooden building
is a fleeting addition, a building that once held worshippers whose
ancestors were taken with the idea of death, resurrection, and
eternal life, and so sat in wooden pews one day a week, perhaps
looking out the stained glass windows as everything got quiet
for a moment, quiet enough to hear blood pulsing, quiet enough
to hear where the river begins in the mountains, quiet enough
to hear the light landing in the treetops.

Highway Prayer

I find myself looking through the rectangle of the window
hearing a voice from outside, low and indecipherable,
recognizing only that it's human, and then hear the shifting
sound of truck engines and the steady hum of tires
on pavement, how many circles the wheels must make each
day, the perfect plunging of pistons, rubber touching the road,
the vehicle plowing through the world,
making unseen ripples in the air.

The Book of 'O'

after a book by Kai Chan made of mussel shells

We are always gathering things up,
walking along and trying to remember
what it was we were dreaming or thinking.
We lift up an eons-old rock from the shore,
or the bone of a long-dead animal,
or seed pods or egg cases. We are collectors
who want to hold on to the remnants of this world
and make something out of it. We see the mussel shells
dropped by the gulls on the ledges. All around us barnacles
are opening and closing sending their delicate
fans into the ocean, the same ocean that passed
through the mussel, the same ocean that was our home,
which is why we're so eager to baptize ourselves in it,
to scurry around its edges and grab what lives in it,
so that in some way it might live in us.

All we're grabbing is memory. After the gull
has eaten the mussel, we hold the emptiness in our hands,
like a book that's already been read, like a museum
of light and energy. We want to read this book,
which is the bible of the ocean. In the beginning
there was water and the mussel said, "let there be water
and let there be enough rock to hold onto." And there was.
And the mussel said, "let the ocean drift in and out of my body
so that we are one, water and flesh." And it was so.
And the mussel said, "let my spawn travel in the water
and drift among the granite." This is how the mussel
made the world, only it didn't have a name for itself.
Back then it was called the filter of all things,
since the world passed through it twice a day.

This is the book that would be too long to write in words,
so the mussel made a shell to tell the story,

and built the shadow of itself inside it, inscribed the line
where the ocean meets the edge of the land,
the water rises and falls. You'd like to place it
in all the hotels and motels for lonely travelers to consider,
after they've surfed through 40 channels of nothing,
even the Weather Channel and Home Shopping Network and they open
the nightstand drawer, moments away from despair
or room service and there it is: The small book made of shells.
It's not the only story, but it's the whole story,
the story of its making, the whisper of the tide,
the birds circling overhead, for whom there is another book,
one that floats and flutters, hovers and plummets.

Evening Prayer

If each serious thought is a prayer then I'm praying now,
praying as I look at the thin tops of the locust trees across
the road, the spring just coming on, whatever life force drives
through the cells of the wood, the bark, the roots
all at work now as I'm looking at it, not in relationship with it,
but at least taking it in, just as I'm taking in the day turning
to night, each day the spinning Earth, the third
from the Sun in the order of the planets I memorized
in second grade, even Pluto way out at the end of the line,
which now they tell us may not even be a planet.
Well to me it is, rotating in the icy reaches,
where there is no such word as horizon or atmosphere,
while on my horizon this evening, Planet Earth, clouds
are gathering, new clouds, clouds full of rain
to be praised and sung about.

Learning to Dance

My sister had to teach me to clap out the beats
of *Pretty Little Angel Eyes* even though rhythm
should pulse through your body as sure as your heart beat,
but we have to re-learn it, on Friday dance classes
with Mr. Parsons, who we saw adjusting his toupee
in the boys bathroom before he went to the gym.
The cha-cha, the jitterbug, the fox trot– all those steps
just to get close to girls. Once you can dance you can
teach yourself to feel the beats of the world
that all grow out of your own heart, thrumming
underneath you like a furnace in the basement, and the slow
beat of the earth turning, and the small staccato of leaf and wind.
At first I listen, and then place the numbered footsteps out in front of me,
to know the pattern of my dance. Arthur Murray is
standing by like some guardian angel or perhaps like
the angel Jacob wrestled with—*I will not let you go
until you bless me*—I whisper to Arthur,
who has already closed all his dance schools, his business
failed. *I will not let you go until you show me the next
steps in the world*—the locomotion, the line dance, some
sort of two-step that will allow me to celebrate, like Zorba
dancing, like someone ecstatic, a dervish, someone dancing
for joy, joy alone, a whole body moving in celebration over
a breathing world, as if you could dance the world into a different
song, dance from cradle to grave, slow dance
with your own soul, the close breath, the hot skin
against hot skin, the bodies pulling away as the music stops.
This is how we learn to move, one step at a time, each step
like a breath in the world of motion and we capture slow time,
we turn in a circle and see our ancestors and our future,
we see T.S. Eliot looking for the still point, a sad man in a suit,
who needs to loosen his tie and jitterbug, who needs to cut up
his poems and spin on one foot, the way the Temptations could,
the song as much about movement as lyrics, the song about
all of us moving together, for once, as one.

Prayer for What is Lost

We are moving forward
or in some direction up,
down, east, west, to the side,
down the canyon walls,
watching the light fall
on the cliffs, which makes
the light seem ancient because
the red stone is hundreds
of millions of years old,
but the light is from today,
it is what the plants are moving
out of the earth to meet,
it heats the air that lifts the birds
that float and hover
over what is made from now.

Psalm

The only psalm I had memorized was the 23rd
and now I find myself searching for the order
of the phrases knowing it ends with *surely*
goodness and mercy will follow me
all the days of my life and I will dwell
in the house of the Lord forever only I remember
seeing a new translation from the original Hebrew
and forever wasn't forever but *a long time*
which is different from forever although
even a long time today would be
good enough for me even a minute entering
the House would be good enough for me,
even a hand on the door or dropping today's
newspaper on the stoop or looking in the windows
that are reflecting this morning's clouds in first light.

Listening to the Music

After an assembled guitar by Bobby Hansson

We all make things, but sometimes what we are doing
is making things obvious, or too obvious. You want
to make them obvious enough. You want to take the neck
of an Epiphone guitar and add a 16mm film canister and strings
and all of a sudden you're making music.
You want to find the one thing and add it to another.
You want to look in the trashcan to find out what's
been lost and then introduce it to your old friends—words,
sounds, and dreams—and see if they can make a marriage.
Your artistic life is dating all the time, trying to imagine
itself in love, or at least living together for a while,
trying to imagine a life inside an apartment and what
every morning is like, drinking coffee and looking out the window.
I don't know where the muses are. I did see them on the top
of a theater in Mexico once, but I think there is something
calling out from the broken necks of old guitars,
from the fragment of a label that could say *icy* or *spicy*
or the rivets that you can use to join things together to make
something instrumental. We are building and interpreting.
We write the poem and wait to see if it sings,
like if you hum the right note, everything in the room that can
will vibrate with it, the piano, the glasses, and the pipes,
a harmony made out of the unexpected.
The unexpected and disregarded, like Emma Lazarus who
is calling to all objects, like Jesus is on the Mount asking
for the poor, the downtrodden, the forgotten and the discarded.
This is where the new life comes from: metal, wood, breath and sound,
the imagination is in the thing itself; it's imagining its own life,
making its own communion, breaking bread with the world,
embracing what's left us. The imagination is plucking
on the taut strings of today, it's putting its fingers down
on the old fret board, it's making a sound that's traveling,
circling the ear, the nautilus chamber, entering

into the tiny bones that vibrate against your skull, it's waiting
to see if someone is listening. That's the sound to wait for.

Wake Up Prayer

When I rise in the dark before dawn
and move my head quickly to the side
I see a flash of light behind my eyes
as if this is the inner light that is
flickering inside me all the time,
in the night when I am on automatic pilot
and moving between the dead and the living
or in the day when I am hearing the animal world call
to me, the crows announcing the sun rising,
the clouds moving across the celestial dome
that makes itself blue in my eyes
although if I were another species I'd be perceiving
this landscape in a different way and we are surely
all seeing our worlds in our own ways,
from the eternity of mountains that once led
another life underwater, to the molten life
of our souls, heated beneath the surface, ready
for action, ready every morning for the call.

If We Are All Going to Die, Beautifully or Not

If we're all going to pass away, which we surely are,
then each moment is precious, each movement of my watch
the digital reminder that Time's winged chariot
is gathering up all the hours, minutes, seconds,
all the ticks and tocks, and heading straight off into oblivion.
Oblivion, where we started and where we are headed,
our long sleep in the dust. The fish wakes up one morning
and goes out for a swim in the marsh grass,
a day like any other, dorsal fin twisting slightly, gills flapping,
when the quick strike of the great blue heron changes everything
from water to air to light. This is when one kind of energy becomes
another, when sun becomes plankton becomes fish flesh,
becomes bird in flight. The heron makes its croaking sound,
its dream-like big flap of wings and heads off to an island where
its rookery makes enough shit to kill the trees.
Speaking of destroying islands, we're doing that pretty
well ourselves, unable to have a longer view than today.
And we have so many todays:
The today of our own front door, the today of our history,
the today of rain falling, and the today of our heart beating,
which is the rhythm of the whole planet. If we're so tied
to everything, how can we have moved so far away from it?
At sunset we watch the river empty past deserted mill buildings
into the ocean. What strange beauty as the red light
reflects on the bricks. The strange beauty of ugliness,
which may be related, scientists and researchers think,
to the strange beauty of death. Free at last, free at last,
which is great for you and me if we're ready,
but how about all those who aren't ready to shuffle
off the stage, who aren't ready to enter into the heron's sharp beak.
Ready or not, the moment arrives behind the wheel of a car,
or in the hospital bed or in the too-deep water.
When you're younger death grabs your stomach
with the shock of disbelief, but then it begins to walk
behind you, and then closer, perhaps next to you for a while,

until he puts his arms around you one day. This is the day,
you think, as if you'll remember this day the way you'd remember
the day you were born, when you emerged out of the birth canal
into the world that touched your body with light and dust.

In Praise of Hands

It's not just the people
who live in the city

who've lost the thread
that ties them to the woven

world of stones and earth,
fields alive with pollen and wings.

Who among us understands
how oceans rise and fall,

currents swirling around the planet
with messages in bottles

floating on the water.
When the tide is out

we can go to the shore
dig clay with our bare hands

and make something beautiful from it,
a vessel with thin walls

that holds a canyon.
In both hands, like an offering,

we can hold the memory
of eroded stones and earth,

eons contained in this empty bowl.
We can fill it with water

that reflects the sky that has
witnessed everything since

time began, we can drink and be blessed,
clouds gathering over us.

Finding Home

The road map home isn't neatly folded
as if I never need to look at it.
I'm always referring to it,
partly opened on the passenger's seat,
fluttering with the breeze coming in the window,

creased white at the edges, beginning
to tear where it has been awkwardly
refolded so many times. I need to consult
the black lines, the yellow clusters around
the cities, the detailed inset to remind myself

I remember the way. I know that it's not safe
to drive this way. If I stop looking at the map
and just keep my eyes on the road, I'll realize
the directions are part of my body,
moving inside my veins and arteries, blood coursing

back and forth on the highways of the heart,
the tattered histories in the creases of my brain,
the small paths inscribed on the folds of my eyelids.
I'm a tattooed man, a marked man,
everything written inside me, like the space capsules

sent out to communicate with different worlds,
with all the essential symbols contained within:
music, a page from a sacred text, essential equations,
something about carbon and oxygen, messages
that light years away can be deciphered and understood.

Snow Globe

A man wakes inside a snow globe.
He shakes back and forth, jumps
up and down and the snow begins
to fall with a light snowflake flutter
and drift that covers everything, making
perfect outlines on the branches of trees
while ropes of snow drop suddenly
from where they've piled up on the power lines
making an *I Ching* hexagram of snow that
descends and vanishes. The man can't tell
the future through these divinations,
but he begins to look at this white world,
which has the quiet of memory. He recognizes
his own town, where he begins to wander.
His boot prints get covered up as he walks
past small stores that don't exist anymore,
barber shops with comic books where
clipped hairs gather in the stapled creases,
butcher shops with sawdust on the floor
and he knows that this is a world that is
vanishing and has vanished. He looks
to the rooftops where the snow reduces
everything to geometry, squares and rectangles,
as if there is a pattern to the world
that the snow is making visible.
The man finds his house and walks up the steps.
The snow has settled on his collar. He shakes
himself as he walks, more snow falls all around.
He climbs the stairs and finds his bed. The snow
is falling in his room. It makes a blanket for him
and he lies down. Outside the plow trucks
have started their rounds. He can see
the amber light flashing through the window
and hear the plow blades scrape the pavement.
It has grown late now and the truck's headlights

pierce the darkness. He can see into the cabs
of the trucks, where the drivers
are going about their jobs, their blaze orange
caps on their heads, jackets smelling of exhaust
and cigarettes, keeping things clear.
The man shakes his head as he falls off to sleep.
It will be a long night,
and the crews will be busy.

When I First Heard Noah's Story How God Gave a Sign That the Earth Would Never Be Flooded Again I Had Never Seen a Rainbow

So when it rained hard on the New Jersey streets,
when the rain made little domes as it struck the asphalt
and torrents rushed down by the curbs
and into the storm sewer, the rainbows appeared.
The illuminated oil slicks, God's multi-colored promise,
shone on the streets, floating on puddles
glistening on the wet blacktop.
The world was new again and water
was dripping off the leaves of the sheltering maples.
God was in Heaven and I was riding
my bike, fast, through the puddles.
There were no doves with olive branches,
but their relatives, the pigeons,
slapped their wings as they left the earth
and banked gracefully in unison.
And how far off was I with the rainbows?
Weren't the oil slicks a kind of covenant
that had traveled from the 4.6 billion-year-old sun
down to the earth, growing prehistoric plants
that rose again as oil and powered and lubricated
the engines of Fords and Buicks?
May I be forgiven for misinterpreting
an old story. It was all I knew
and I was making the best of it.

Mr. Fix-It

My father never made anything or
fixed anything, even though we had
the obligatory tools in the basement,
the beautiful hand drill that belonged

to my great grandfather the carpenter,
the once-used brushes and the mysterious
cans of paint and shellac. And he never
cooked anything either, never turned

the coffee pot down to perk,
never cracked an egg and only once
that I remember barbecued steaks,
the smoke rising to heaven like a burnt offering

from the charred remains. When he returned
home at night, the smell of gas and oil
still close to his clothes, he'd settle on the couch
finishing a *New York Times* crossword puzzle while

keeping track of the Yankees on TV, until he
fell asleep, only to rouse when I'd change the channel.
"I was watching that," he'd mumble, though asleep,
and I'd believe him, but now I think he wasn't there

but had been at his domestic work, the night shift,
dreaming the lives of his children,
building a house of words, writing
the perfect story whose ending we never get to.

Leaving Home: Route 2 from Maine to Vermont

for Wesley McNair

This two-lane road road knits
the North together, where each town

in each state is more alike than different,
and you enter into river valleys where

the vapor from the paper mills condenses
into huge clouds, as if this is the place

where clouds are manufactured and sent
out into the world. Today a shipment

of cumulus is floating by,
making its passage over the woods

that encroach on the worn fields, over
the trailers next to the farm houses,

over the satellite dishes and churches,
the car dealers and beauty salons,

the deer in the woods, and the stubble from
last year's corn barely covered with snow.

Each town is alike, but driving through
Mercer, Maine reminds me

that we are all from someplace in particular,
and I take note. Spotting a sign that says

Town Line Redemption
I write it down while I'm trying to steer,

thinking this is not about returning empty
bottles, this is about what fills us, how

we are in love with leaving a place or in love
with staying, how we are saved by

coming home and by going away. We walk
outside our houses to begin our journey, near or far.

Opening a door, closing a door:
this is where the story begins.

Home

My soul has been leaving
my body at night.

I'd like to think
that it has been traveling

around the world fluttering
from door to door

feeding the hungry
embracing angry people until

all their hate dissipates
and only love remains

or gathering up weapons and burying them
to rust in the sand.

But I don't know where it goes,
only that when I awoke before dawn

my hips and knees
ached with its re-entry

as if I had been walking all day.
Outside something was howling

or singing a thin song
and the two of us

rested again until morning
each dreaming the other's life.

Now

The moment
bitterness leaves,
your heart
is so light
it floats down the street
and drifts
to a dark
field in spring,
waiting for its
one moment
and the rain of love.

Notes & Acknowledgments

Acknowledgments are due to the editors of the following publications, in whose pages some of the poems in this book first appeared.

Litany, Prayer, Prayer in the Strip Mall, Bangor Maine, Grief Arrives in Its Own Time, Water Prayer, and *Prayer for Slowing Down* appeared in The Sun

Silence appeared in Bangor Metro

If We're All Going to Die Beautifully or Not appeared in Café Review

For Alice, Who Taught Me About Poems and *When I First Heard Noah's Story* appeared in Eggemoggin Reach Review.

With thanks to Wesley McNair and Betsy Sholl for reading the manuscript, to Kim Stafford, whose 'run-on sentence' assignment during a workshop at Haystack engendered a whole series of poems, and to the Vermont Studio Center and the Haystack Mountain School of Crafts for providing the time and the places to write.

Thanks to my wife Susan and sons Isaac and Samuel for their wisdom, humor, and encouragement.

Stuart Kestenbaum grew up in Maplewood, New Jersey and received a B.A. degree from Hamilton College. He has lived in Maine for many years and since 1988 has been the director of the Haysack Mountain School of Crafts in Deer Isle. He is also the author of *Pilgrimage* (Coyote Love Press) and *House of Thanksgiving* (Deerbrook Editions). He is married to visual artist Susan B. Webster and they have two children, Isaac and Samuel, who are all grown up now.